Why Do We Have Seasons?

Sara L. Latta

Enslow Elementary

an imprint of

 Enslow Publishers, Inc.

40 Industrial Road
Box 398
Berkeley Heights, NJ 07922
USA

http://www.enslow.com

Words to Know

hibernate (HY bur nayt)—To spend the winter sleeping or resting.

migrate (MY grayt)—To move from one place to another.

season (SEE zuhn)—One of the four parts of the year. Each season has a certain kind of weather.

tilt—To lean to one side.

Earth is tilted.

Contents

What is Spring?

Spring is one of the four seasons of the year. The other seasons are summer, fall, and winter. Each season lasts about three months. In spring, signs of warmer weather are everywhere!

winter

fall

summer

spring

Why Do we have seasons?

Earth goes around the sun. One trip around the sun makes a year. During this trip, Earth tilts to one side.

Spring in north part of Earth

Summer

North Pole tilts toward the sun; it is summer in the north part of Earth.

Winter

The tilt causes more or less sunlight to fall on different parts of Earth.

Earth's path around sun

In winter, Earth's North Pole points away from the sun. As Earth moves around the sun, the North Pole begins to tilt toward the sun. This is when spring begins.

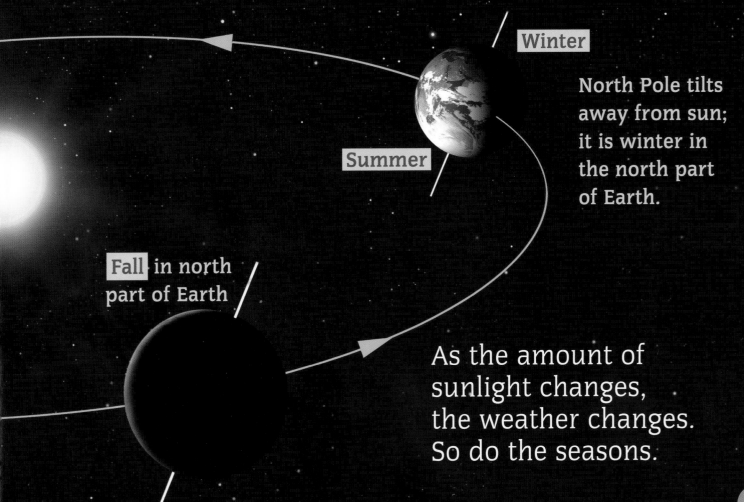

Winter

North Pole tilts away from sun; it is winter in the north part of Earth.

Summer

Fall in north part of Earth

As the amount of sunlight changes, the weather changes. So do the seasons.

When Does Spring Begin?

Spring comes after winter. The first day of spring in the north part of Earth is around March 21.

The north part of Earth slowly gets more heat from the sun. The days begin to get warmer. The daytime also begins to get longer. The days seem longer because the sun is out later.

Spring often brings rainy weather. You may see a rainbow after a spring shower.

What are the first signs of spring?

Warmer, longer days help plants and seeds grow. Flowers pop up to brighten the snow and dark ground. Tiny green leaves appear on the trees. New grass begins to grow again.

What Do Animals Do in the Spring?

grey squirrel

Animals feel the warmer weather and longer days, too. Animals that hibernate in the winter, like bears, wake up. They are very hungry! They like to eat the young plants that grow in the spring. The food helps them get strong again.

grizzly bear cub

13

When are animals Born?

Many animal babies are born in the spring. The new plants give the babies and parents fresh food to eat. They will eat and grow during spring and summer.

baby striped skunks

Eastern cottontail baby rabbits

Why Do animals migrate?

Many animals cannot stay warm or find food in the cold. Where winter weather is too cold, the animals migrate south. It is warmer there.

Snow geese migrate.

When it is warm again in the spring, many animals migrate back north. The return of the robins is one of the first signs of spring in the north parts of the United States.

American robin, male

What Do People Do in the Spring?

Farmers and gardeners plant seeds in the spring. The rain and warm sun will make their vegetables and flowers grow. Spring has sprung! What will *you* do?

EXPERIMENT

MY SHADOW

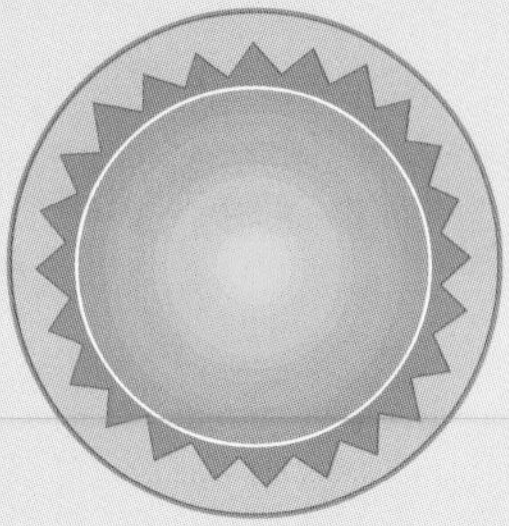

You will need:

- **sidewalk chalk, 3 colors**
- **a helper**
- **a bright sunny day**

1. Pick a bright sunny day. Early in the morning, stand outside in a place that will be sunny all day long. Ask a helper to trace your shadow with sidewalk chalk. Have them trace around your feet so that you

can stand in the same spot later on. Lie down next to your shadow. Is it taller or shorter than you are? Where is the sun in the sky?

2. Around noon that same day, stand in the same spot. Ask your friend to trace your shadow with a different color of chalk. How has your shadow changed? Where is the sun now?

3. Do the same thing late in the afternoon. Notice how your shadow changes as the sun moves across the sky.

4. The time of day when your shadow was shortest was when the sun's rays were most direct. During the different seasons, some places on earth get more direct sunlight, and some less direct sunlight.

Learn More

Books

Esbaum, Jill. *Everything Spring.* Washington, D.C.: National Geographic Children's Books, 2010.

Rissman, Rebecca and Siân Smith. *Spring.* Chicago, Ill.: Heinemann-Raintree, 2009.

Smith, Siân. *Changing Seasons.* Chicago, Ill.: Heinemann-Raintree, 2009.

Learn More

Enchanted Learning: Spring Crafts
<http://www.enchantedlearning.com/crafts/spring/>
Creative and enchanting children's crafts for springtime.

Monarch Butterfly: Journey North: Kids Page
<http://www.learner.org/jnorth/tm/monarch/jr/
KidsJourneyNorth.html>
Learn about the life cycle and Spring migration of Monarch
butterflies.

Kaboose: Spring recipes and ideas
<http://holidays.kaboose.com/spring/>
Spring crafts and recipes for children.

Index

Enslow Elementary, an imprint of Enslow Publishers, Inc.

Enslow Elementary® is a registered trademark of Enslow Publishers, Inc.

Copyright © 2012 by Enslow Publishers, Inc.

All rights reserved.

No part of this book may be reproduced by any means without the written permission of the publisher.

Original edition published as *What Happens in Spring* in 1996.

Library of Congress Cataloging-in-Publication Data

Latta, Sara L.
   Why is it spring? / Sara L. Latta.
      p. cm. — (Why do we have seasons?)
   Rev. ed. of: What happens in spring? 1996.
   Includes index.
   ISBN 978-0-7660-3986-5
   1. Spring–Juvenile literature. 2. Seasons–Juvenile
literature. I. Latta, Sara L. What happens in spring? II. Title.
   QB637.5.L38 2012
   508.2–dc23   2011019297
Paperback ISBN 978-1-59845-389-8
ePUB ISBN 978-1-4645-0482-2
PDF ISBN 978-1-4646-0482-9

Printed in the United States of America.

092011 Lake Book Manufacturing, Inc., Melrose Park, IL

10 9 8 7 6 5 4 3 2 1

To Our Readers: We have done our best to make sure all Internet Addresses in this book were active and appropriate when we went to press. However, the author and the publisher have no control over and assume no liability for the material available on those Internet sites or on other Web sites they may link to. Any comments or suggestions can be sent by e-mail to comments@enslow.com or to the address on the back cover.

♻ Enslow Publishers, Inc., is committed to printing our books on recycled paper. The paper in every book contains 10% to 30% post-consumer waste (PCW). The cover board on the outside of each book contains 100% PCW. Our goal is to do our part to help young people and the environment too!

Note to Parents and Teachers: The Why Do We Have Seasons? series supports the National Science Education Standards for K–4 science. The Words to Know section introduces subject-specific vocabulary words, including pronunciation and definitions. Early readers may need help with these new words.

Photo Credits: © Corel Corporation, pp. 20–23; © 2011 Photos.com, a division of Getty Images. All rights reserved, pp. 4, 5, 8, 9–19; Mark Garlick/ Science Photo Library, pp. 20–23; Shutterstock, p. 2.

Cover Photo: © 2011 Photos.com, a division of Getty Images. All rights reserved.

Science Consultant, Harold Brooks, PhD, NOAA/National Severe Storms, Laboratory, Norman, Oklahoma

Series Literacy Consultant, Allan A. De Fina, PhD, Dean, College of Education/ Professor of Literacy Education, New Jersey City University, Past President of the New Jersey Reading Association